INSTANT
MESSAGES

INSTANT MESSAGES

The Print Project
P. O. Box 703
Bearsville, NY 12409
connect@instantmessageslgm.com

Distributed to the book trade by:
Independent Publishers Group
814 North Franklin Street
Chicago, IL 60610
(312) 337–0747

Design: Elizabeth Cline
Graphics: by the author
Graphics on pages 4, 34, 37, 42, 74, 80 collaboration with Howard Blume

FIRST EDITION
ISBN-13: 978-0-9976991-0-4
ISBN-10: 0-9976991-0-8

Instant Messages no more sly cupped hand palming crumpled
secrets between those old wooden desks Shaping we shape our
minds in monologue is that really true? we wonder...Pluck a Line
from the torrent of data and the wat fall of wisdom you pluck
a line or two, a boggle of words that somehow captures all the
distinctions in a dense nugget, a moment of heavy matter that
draws' everything that made it into itself. That's all you remem-
ber. A Thought If you sit You will have a thought. From among
the Infinite possible thoughts---your thought. Words Coming
From Is it a paradox or perfectly normal that words come best
from silence? Body of Water me busy breezy body of water
when the waves flatten to glass then my bottom my rocks my
sad-eyed fish

INSTANT
MESSAGES

lowellgm

Not that we
front still, ancient law applies: the more there is in front the
less you find
very clever
the very
battle is
Wander up and down an unfamiliar street. Look for a clearing. By
and by the signal will find you. This Place Too tired for telepathy
we read and drink in illuminated nights. Suddenly wow, our brains,
the ability to talk! Ugu
have all the apps you need! Head Line Animal Behavior Follows
Dopamine Habit Science Researchers claim it takes only ten
casual whacks to carve a habit's permanent tracks across your
helpless brain I Tried I tried to change....I tried to break the bad
habits...but just couldn't...stop myself! Addiction Tension one
part says use Easy To See You, rights, dreams, ambitions, and
your own little feelings...But here you are: you're not creative.
You're middling. It's easy to see, why you'd wind up turning to
drink and drugs and whatever. Other You wonder why The other
is so other Even butt up against it You feel separated, alone,
Conversing...Interesting story...Here's one of mine, even better !
Delayed Reaction long before global arming we used to drive to
New York near sunset marveling at the brown and purple sky. Not

the print
project

Birds Words are not birds
call, despite what some
thought from branch to b
tiny heart Motion Preferred in the atmosphere...still sky, silent
leaves, not so much fun Happy the happy pretend there is no end
The Sad The sad may take heart it will all be forgot Trouble In
the Country The mockingbird has learned to imitate our alarm-
clock From Another Realm In the tailwind of her passing, a
strange sensation, flora and decay. Just because there's no odor
doesn't mean there's no scent. Even a dog can explain that. Too
Bad what you said you said what you did you did. can't unsay
can't undo Predators Predators Attack By Mouth Milkmaids

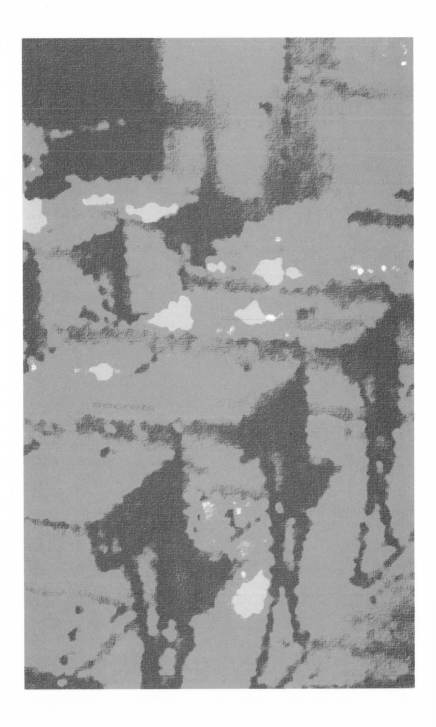

Instant Messages

no more

sly cupped hand

palming crumpled

secrets between

those old

wooden desks

Shaping

we shape

our minds

in monologue

is that

really true?

we wonder...

Pluck a Line

from the torrent of data

you pluck a line or two,

a boggle of words that somehow

captures all the distinctions

in a dense nugget, a moment

of heavy matter that draws

everything that made it

into itself.

Pluck the line.

That's all you

remember.

INSTANT MESSAGES   LOWELL MILLER

A Thought

If you sit
you will have
a thought.

From among the
infinite possible thoughts
---your thought.

Crib of World

In the crib of world

dead blankets and plastic

toys, torn animals...

a tooth-scraped nook

dim light day and night...

no bling here

no video crew

no babes, no rides---

watch where you put

your hands

there b. bomb triggers

and sensors

all random shit

Four Bars

Keep waving
it around.
Wander up
and down an
unfamiliar street.
Look for a clearing.
By and by
the signal
will find you.

where you want to be
on the spectrum

The Problem

The problem
of where you
want to be
on the spectrum

Front / Back

Not that we

don't want front

we do want front

we must have front

still, ancient law applies:

the more there is in front

the less you find in back

My Opinion

It's a cozy thing
It tells me who I am
Yes, I may change it
But not without a fight.

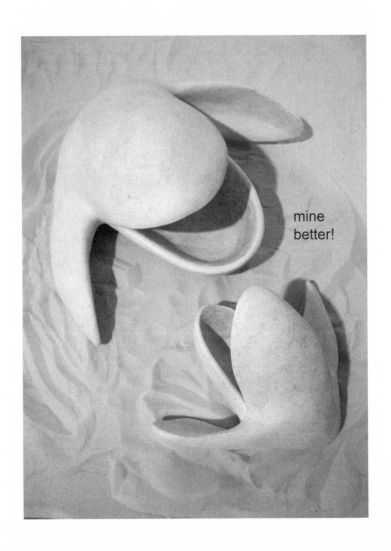

mine
better!

Conversing...

Interesting story...
Here's one of mine,
even better!

Up

Up

at 4:00 a.m.

can't sleep

so little

time

left...

Happy

the happy

pretend

there is no end

Old Age

his face gone

hollow, lips

pale as worms

nothing

turned out

as he thought

it would...

Him By Himself

She didn't quite know
why she loved him
as he lay under a plank
of sun in the morning,
blankets kicked down
across his thighs

She heard a kind of low
murmur or mumbling
as she gazed, there,
him by himself, a language
she could not make out,
a message just out of reach.

CAN'T UNSAY
CAN'T UNDO

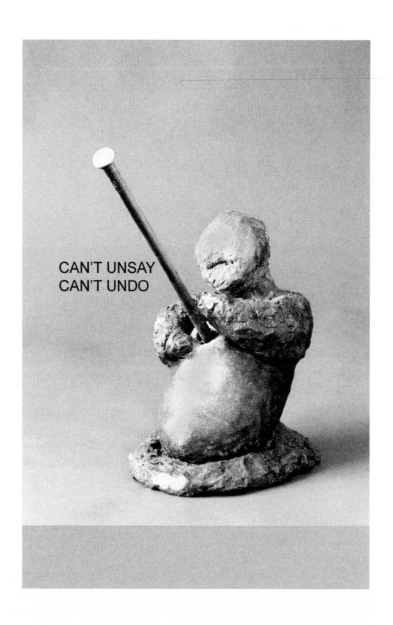

Too Bad

what you said
you said

what you did
you did.

can't unsay
can't undo

Counters

That clicking sound

all around---

definitely not

your imagination.

It's the counters---

their keypads, their mices

their silent devices

Tivo!

if u no tivo

it is gone

if u no tivo

then woe

it is gone

it is all gone

Spirituality Update

Look deep

within that screen:

your bundle comes

with all the apps

you need...

Emily Dicks

had her tricks

nothing wasted

nothing feigned

I was sure
I would
remember

Something I Forgot

something I

forgot

I was sure

I would remember

must be

my fookin brain

agin

ESP Comes Soon

When all the apps

are written, and robots

mimic every move

ESP be coming next---

but you already knew that

Could Be

Spinoza was a lens-grinder.

That spikey-haired chick

showing high-fashion frames

in Sunglass Hut...

a new paradigm

encrypted in her tats?

You never know

who's working on what...

Oceanfront Balcony

Many clinical studies have shown
the physical eye itself relaxes
gives it up and goes off guard
in the presence of a long horizon

today he was wondering
how his life would have been different,
if there'd been the big view
every morning, from airy
balcony or quiet living room

What if there'd been the big view every morning?

Meme of Here

But we know...
there's more than here

We sense a spacious room
next door, beyond that wall---
somber oriental rugs mat the floor
beneath carved mahogany tables.
You can hear muffled sounds
from the other side---
male conversations, clinking tableware,
decks of cards expertly shuffled
but that room has no door...
How to get over there?
How to be present.
in the here and there?

Illusion of Individuality

no one can be you.

you bend with millions

over page or screen

absorbing the exact same information

in the exact same instant

still you feel like the only one.

Notice

Repent!
Messiah
might be
anyone!

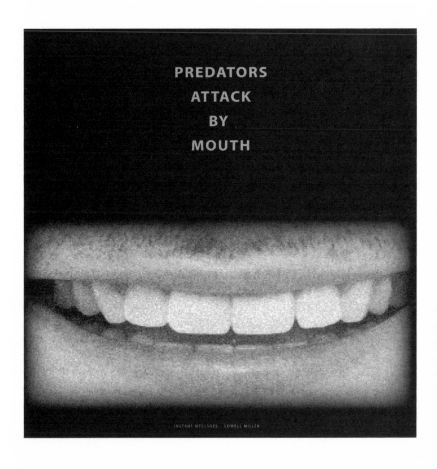

PREDATORS
ATTACK
BY
MOUTH

INSTANT MESSAGES LOWELL MILLER

Predators

Predators

Attack

By

Mouth

Words Coming From

Is it a paradox
or perfectly normal
that words come
best from silence?

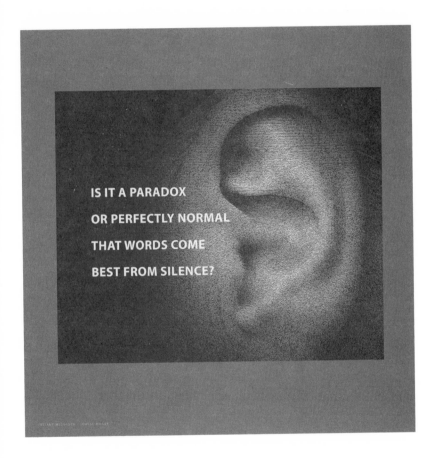

IS IT A PARADOX
OR PERFECTLY NORMAL
THAT WORDS COME
BEST FROM SILENCE?

Not Birds

Words
are not birds
and so
they don't trill
or whistle
or call, despite
what some believe

Still, they're flying
transparent
thought
from branch
to branch
no wings
no air
no rapidly beating
tiny heart

Tracks

those tracks

in the aging snow

where you were

where you went

white on white

disclosed in shadow

snow on snow

still white

though not quite

Motion Preferred

in the atmosphere...

still sky,

silent leaves,

not so much fun

Talk and Worry

talk and worry

blots out eros

this we know

but doesn't stop us

DON'T TAKE IT
PERSONALLY
YOU'RE JUST
ONE MORE
EXAMPLE

Poet Said

A poet said

I feel this

I feel that

I remember

me mum and me da.

And why should we care?

Don't take it

personally---

You're just

one more

example!

The Problem of Society

Man puts on
a hat,
forgets he's
wearing it.

man puts on
a hat
forgets he's
wearing it

Milkmaids

Milkmaids were milking
me everywhere
the little bells
on their slippers
made a tinkling carpet
of sound. One stood
in front and milked
me dry. One took me
behind a tree and arched
her body into mine
one grabbed me
from my back and milked
me roughly did
she wear a mask?
The yard was filled
with milkmaids
but I only had
so much to give

Taskmaster

Awake, there is

a list of tasks

like stepping stones

On the last stone

a new list

he slipped in

while you were

sleeping

Every Damn Day

saw this

saw that

felt

ate this

ate that

slept

The Great Debate

It's just you

and your opinions

vs.

me and my opinions

We become

an adamant and relentless

outpouring of words

until the very end.

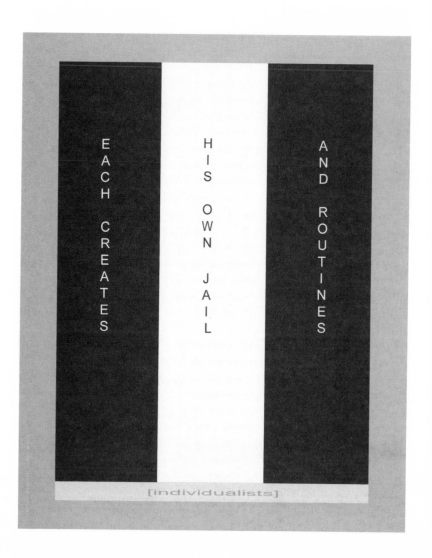

EACH CREATES HIS OWN JAIL AND ROUTINES

[individualists]

Individualists

Each creates

his own

jail

and routines

Be An Artist

Why be an artist?

Why not just

hang back and watch,

amorphous and saturated

in the vibrating

landscape?

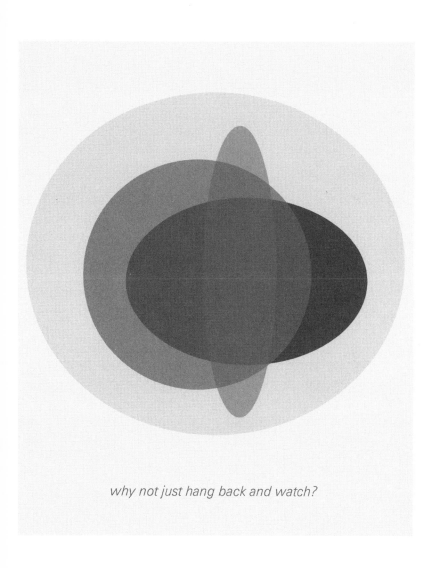

why not just hang back and watch?

Artifact

You need an artifact.

Slip into that high

Intuitive state;

Return with some

Credible evidence.

Doubling

He viewed the line

Of horizon.

It doubled. It

Doubled and doubled.

His eye extended

To the blackest edge.

It doubled and doubled

And doubled and doubled.

He howled

As it doubled.

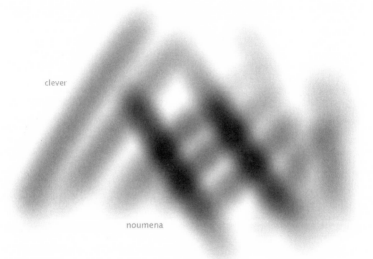

clever

noumena

Around an Armchair

the noumena

are so very clever!

throwing up

opaque landscapes

thwarting all

except the very old

in armchairs

just looking

I Tried

I tried to change…

I tried to break…

…the bad habits…

but just couldn't…

stop myself

Addiction Tension

one

part

says

use

Easy To See

You,
rights, dreams,
ambitions, and your
own little feelings...

But here you are:
you're not creative.
You're middling.
It's easy to see, why you'd
wind up turning
to drink and drugs
and whatever.

Head Line

Animal

Behavior

Follows

Dopamine

Rewards

– Neuroscience Journal, Fall 2014

Habit Science

Researchers claim

it takes only

ten casual whacks

to carve a habit's

permanent tracks

across your helpless brain

Other

You wonder why
The other is so other

Even butt up against it
You feel separated, alone.

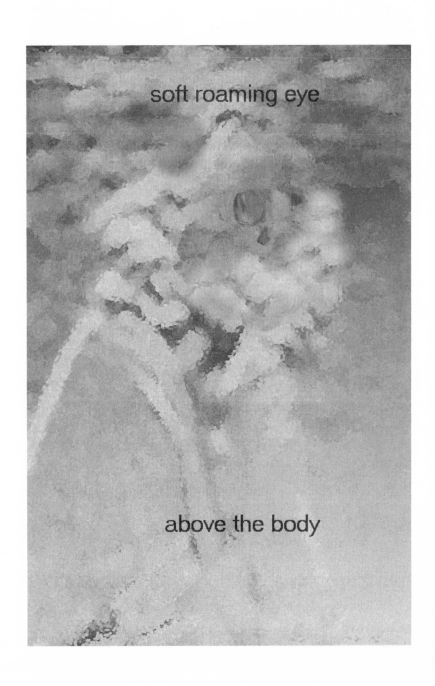

soft roaming eye

above the body

Someone You Know

figures of speech
the soft roaming eye above the body

you come to love
them, the things
and the person, but
as the days die off you find
them hard to measure---

chance crossings,
puzzle parts at the time,
patterns in the random
brought you here
and will take you away...

But you have complete records.
A growing photo stack proves
beyond words;
this is how it was,
it did happen,
it was all correct.

Body of Water

me busy breezy

body of water

when the waves

flatten to glass

then my bottom

my rocks

my sad-eyed fish

my rocks

my sad-eyed fish

Below The Waves

a dark form shudders

deep in ancient water

mud ascends as

unintended clouds

Half The Battle

half

the battle

is trapping

it in

the bottle

From Another Realm

In the tailwind of her

passing, a strange

sensation, flora

and decay.

Just because

there's no odor

doesn't mean

there's no scent.

Even a dog

can explain that.

Popeye, Who Did

look something like
a potato, said
I yam what I yam
and he was.
Who knew Popeye
when he retired
would live not aboard
but in a corner of
your very own
basement
mumbling
puffing
stinking
telling
old stories
to no one
in particular?

DELAYED

REACTION

LONG BEFORE
GLOBAL WARMING
WE USED TO DRIVE
TO NEW YORK
NEAR SUNSET,
MARVELLING AT
THE BROWN AND PURPLE SKY.

Delayed Reaction

long before

global warming

we used to drive

to New York

near sunset

marveling at

the brown and purple sky.

Questions

Half dead and half alive

how is it even possible?

Was it better when

the ratio of years remaining

to years lived

was larger and fatter?

Was it better then?

Afterlife

Yes, there is

an afterlife...

but it is

not fun...

it is like

you are

behind glass

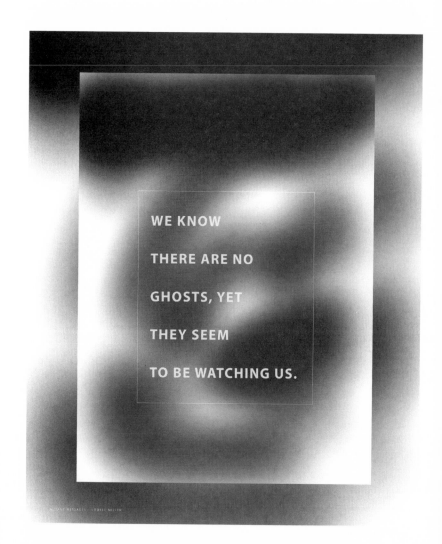

Ghosts

We know

there are no

ghosts, yet

they seem

to be watching us.

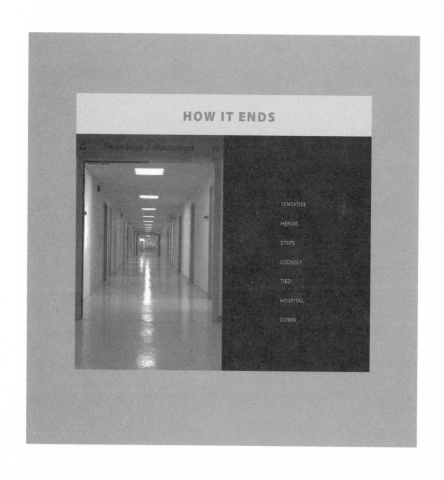

How It Ends

tentative

heroic

steps

loosely

tied

hospital

gown

End of Show

The run is over.

This set will end as kindling

These actors drift, like early man.

What to Do??

Pursue

Aperçus

lowellgm@yahoo.com